The Aminal

by LORNA BALIAN

ABINGDON PRESS

NASHVILLE

THE AMINAL

For Christopher J. and Keith K.

Patrick was having a picnic
all by himself
when he saw it.

Having a picnic all alone is not as pleasant
as having a picnic with a friend.
That's why Patrick decided to catch it
and be a friend to it,
and share his picnic with it,
and take it home with him—
and they would be friends forever.

So he caught it,

and although it tried to hide,
it seemed to be friendly.

Patrick offered to share his picnic,
but the creature wasn't interested in pickles
or peanut-butter sandwiches
or even fig bars.

It only seemed sleepy.

Patrick made a nice soft bed for it,
with grass and dandelion fuzzies, in his lunch bag—
and he started home.

On the way he met Molly.
Patrick told her that he caught an Aminal
all by himself
and that it was sleeping in his lunch bag.

"It's round and green and blinky-eyed
with lots of pricky toenails
and a waggy tail," he said.
"I think it's going to be hungry when it wakes up,
and I have to hurry home and feed it."

And away he went.

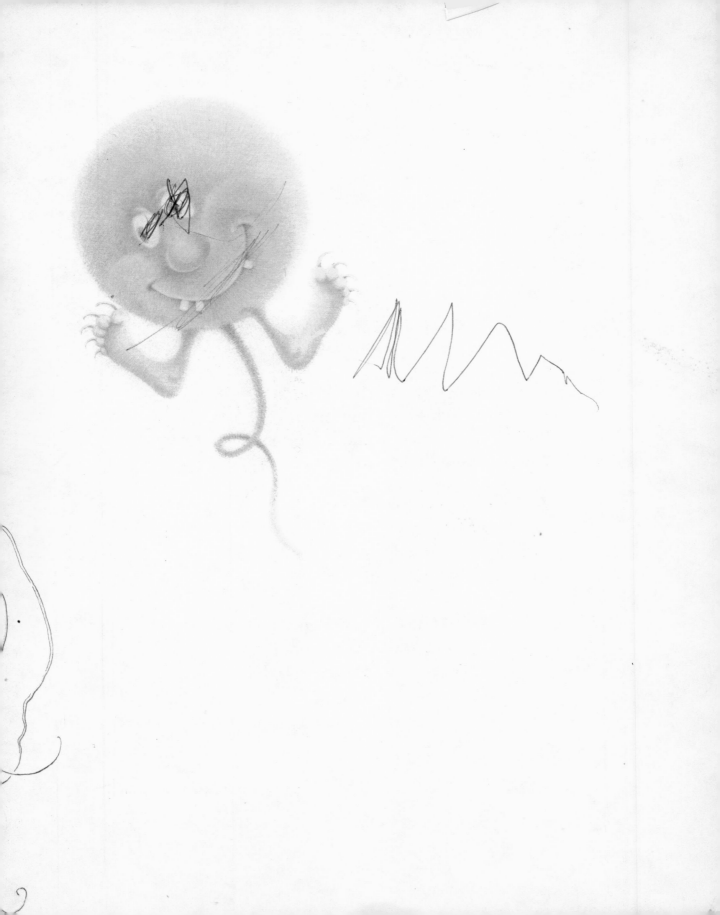

Along came Calvin, who asked Molly
where Patrick was going in such a hurry.
She told him Patrick caught an Aminal
and was going home to feed it.

She said it was a round, wild, green thing
that had slinky eyes,
and lots of toes with prickles on,
and a long waggly tail.

"What does it eat?" he asked.
"I don't know," she said.
"I really can't imagine, Calvin."

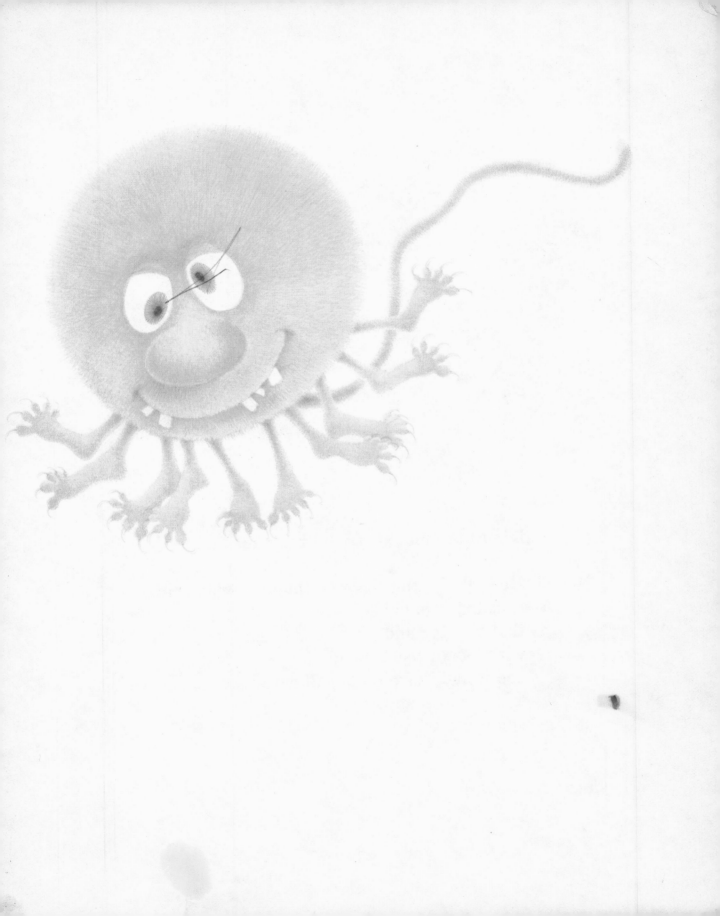

Calvin ran to find his friend Freddie.

He told him that Patrick caught a wild thing
called an Aminal—
that was big and round and green
with lots of feet and eyes,
and it had sharp things all over
and a long snappy tail—
and it ate things!

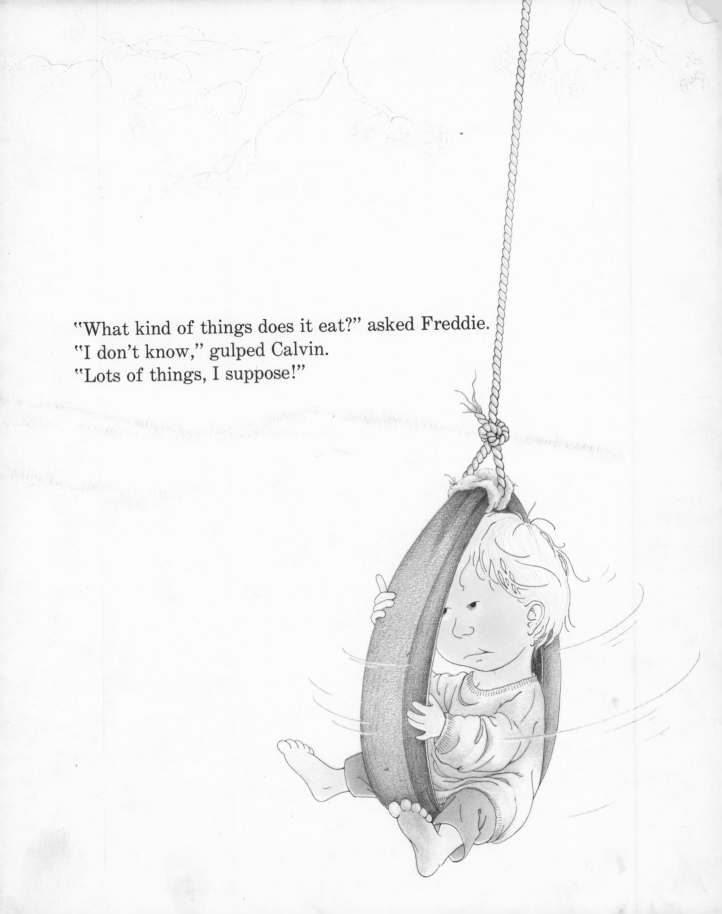

"What kind of things does it eat?" asked Freddie.
"I don't know," gulped Calvin.
"Lots of things, I suppose!"

Freddie told his sister Cookie
about the terrible, wild Aminal thing
that Patrick had caught.

He told her it was BIG and green and furry.
He told her it had eyes and stickery things
all over—and hundreds of feet—
and it had a long tail like a snake
and it ate and ate and ate!

"What does it eat?" gasped Cookie.
"I don't know," said Freddie,
"but it eats lots of it!"
"I wonder what," Cookie whispered.

Cookie told Geraldine that they had better
stay away from Patrick's house because he
had this Aminal thing that was just awful wild,
and although she supposed he kept it locked up—
well, you could never tell what it might do
if it got hungry enough.

She told her it had lots of tangly, stickery, green fur
and terrible eyes—
and it was a hundred feet long—
and it had snakes on its tail!

"How dreadful!" said Geraldine. "What does it eat?"
"What do you think?" whispered Cookie.
"Oh! Dear me!" quivered Geraldine,
feeling very goose-bumpy.

Suddenly it occurred to Cookie
that Patrick was her friend,
that Patrick was little,
that Patrick probably didn't realize
the danger he was in—
that Patrick should be warned,

                    and protected!

They ran to tell the others. . . .

"Patrick is little," Cookie told them.
"Patrick is in danger," she said.
"We have to warn him—and protect him!
He's our friend!"

They all hurried to find something
that might help
to protect a friend . . . .

. . . . and arrived breathlessly at Patrick's house.

"Where is that wild thing you caught, Patrick ?"
they all asked.

"It's behind the house," he replied.
"Do you want to see it?"

Yes, they did—and no—no, they didn't,
but maybe they ought to.
Just a quick peek?
They followed Patrick, fearfully,
around the house.

"It's gone," said Patrick. "IT'S GONE!
It was sitting right here
and now it's gone!

"Help me find it!
Please help me find it!"

They looked in the tall weeds
and found bugs and caterpillars.

They looked in the tree
and found Molly's cat.

Under the bushes they found lots of prickles—
but they weren't green prickles.

They peeked into the garage,
but it was too dark to find anything in there.

They looked everywhere—
Everywhere except . . . .

"THE PORCH!" said Patrick. "Maybe it's hiding under the porch!"

Calvin said he was much too big to crawl under the porch.
Molly was certain she was too big.
Freddie stretched as tall as he could on his tiptoes
and hoped he wouldn't fit in that small dark place.

"I couldn't squeeze under there,"
said Cookie.
Geraldine was sure that
she couldn't either.

But Patrick quickly squirmed under the porch.

I FOUND IT !

I FOUND MY AMINAL !

HERE IT IS !

"Oh, Patrick! That's not an Aminal. That's an ANIMAL!
"A TURTLE animal!" said Calvin, very relieved.

"That's what I said—an Aminal," said Patrick.
"Humph," Geraldine said. "Just a silly little turtle."
"It's a nice friendly little turtle," said Molly.
"What's its name?"
Patrick thought for a moment.
"I didn't name it yet,
but I think I'll call it *Friendly*."

They all agreed that Friendly was a good name

for a friendly little,

harmless little,

green little turtle. . . . .

"What does Friendly eat, Patrick?"
giggled Cookie.

"Mosquitoes," said Patrick. "That's what.
Lots and lots of mosquitoes!"